THIS BOOK IS THE NINTH IN HARPER & ROW'S NATIVE AMERICAN PUBLISHING PROGRAM. ALL PROFITS FROM THIS PROGRAM ARE USED TO SUPPORT PROJECTS DESIGNED TO AID THE NATIVE AMERICAN PEOPLE.

OTHER BOOKS IN THE PROGRAM

Seven Arrows, by Hyemeyohsts Storm

Ascending Red Cedar Moon, by Duane Niatum

Winter in the Blood, by James Welch

Indians' Summer, by Nas'Naga

Carriers of the Dream Wheel, edited by Duane Niatum

Riding the Earthboy 40, by James Welch

Going for the Rain, by Simon Ortiz

The Blood People, by Adolf Hungry Wolf

DIGGING OUT
THE ROOTS

DIGGING OUT THE ROOTS

Poems by
DUANE NIATUM

HARPER & ROW, PUBLISHERS
New York   Hagerstown   San Francisco   London

Library of Congress Cataloging in Publication Data

Niatum, Duane, 1938–
Digging out the roots.
I. Title.
PS3564.I17D5   1977   811'.5'4   76–50453
ISBN 0–06–451155–3 pbk.
ISBN 0–06–451154–5

FIRST EDITION

Designed by Christine Aulicino

Cover painting, "Anapu Luta," by John L. Ihle

Contents

Acknowledgments

The following poems have been published previously in the following books and periodicals, and, where indicated, the author and publisher wish gratefully to acknowledge permission to reprint.

American Poetry Review: "Owl Seen in Rearview Mirror"; "Secret Meeting"; "The Wheel of Return"; "Closing Circles."

Argus (Seattle): "To Awake"; "Celebrating the Center Moon."

Big Moon: "Song to First Woman."

Chicago Review: "The Way." Published under the title "Crow's Way."

Dacotah Territory: "To A Young Woman From Pasco."

Jeopardy: "Digging Out the Roots."

Niagara: "To Love."

Northwest Review: "Reading the Mirrors of the Nameless"; "Fool's Crane Spins the Water Wheel for You."

The Nation: "Separation."

Phoebe: "Poem to a Gypsy Woman."

Poetry Northwest: "Songs from the Maker of Totems."

Poetry Now: "Poems for the Woman Who Fled, No. 1, 2, 3."

Slackwater Review: "The Ruins."

The University of South Dakota Review: "Street Kid"

Spring Rain: "The Hermit."

*Again for those special women,
and the friends still left.*

I.

SONGS FROM THE MAKER OF TOTEMS

Relatives, friends, enemies, will often be harsh,
unfair judges of your life. You may take many paths:
learn from pain, joy, failure. This will matter
little to these people. So listen to your guardian
spirit for directions out of this storm; be grateful
and patient. Because you are young, I, very old,
our village no more, there is little I can say of the
old ways in these bad times. You must grow strong
like mother spruce. You are my son; I leave you
this song.

Francis Patsey, Elder Klallam

SONGS FROM THE MAKER OF TOTEMS

I offer you the chance to forgive your wounds
That often burned down the longhouse.
And you must never blame the village shaker:
I comfort you because of his dreaming.

Watch owl settle in the four directions,
Roost in the fire that burns for salmon's way—
Circle First People who hide in your feelings,
To ease the weight of morning on your eyelids.

Hear the winds give away your pride
In confusion's cave, offer you a light burden,
Seven days of rain, and another storm.

Again, the water dreamers run away with hope:
Thunderbird because he's buried under bone,
Teeth, and shell; Raven because he can't see
Sun touch the crocus beneath the ferns;
Blue Jay because so few hear the humor in his

Laugh, his praise to the women who swim this river;
Whale because he's more hunted than haunted,
Seaweed because it's now mere desert dust.
Beaver because his last dam demolished

The rainbow that sent him off to the stars
Without a cedar chip to find his way home
When the water song fails to hold the summer storm.

Wolf roams the white pine of your terror,
But he'll stop when you stop running behind the dead,

The drummers behind the moon. At dawn, offer him
The wheel, the rattle to shake you to the shore;

It was your ignorance that started the tremor
That fed the sharks closing in;
The suicide stream inching its way to the breakers.

STREET KID

I stand before the window that opens
To a field of sagebrush—
California country northeast of San Francisco.
Holding to the earth and its shield of silence,
The sun burns my thirteen years into the hill.
The white breath of twilight
Whirrs with insects crawling down the glass
Between the bars. But it is the meadowlark
Warbling at the end of the fence
That sets me apart from the rest of the boys,
The cool toughs playing ping pong
And cards before lock-up.
When this new home stops calling on memory,
As well as my nickname, Injun Joe,
Given to me by the brothers,
The Blacks, the Chicanos, the others growing
Lean as this solitude, I step
From the window into the darkness,
Reach my soul building a nest against the wall.

SEPARATION

In
The
Space
Between

My
Shadow
And
Yours

Danced
The
Yellow
Feather
Shield.

O
Woman,
When
You
Left
This
Circle
For
The
Mirror,
Hummingbird
Ran
Away

With
My
Hands.

THE VISITOR

He came to this unknown town to regain his soul,
Ride out the storm with friends he knew were friends,
Follow deer to the river that is quiet in the dawn,
Step softly like wind through wheat, he said.
He wasn't desperate; merely confident there was
No other way he could breathe again while asleep:
His songs were sculptured ghosts, wretched, bloody,
With too many violent roots, nomadic memories,
Burnt-out water drums. He wanted out. Maybe a call
To fiction; some new direction where he might collapse,
Recognize his shadow in tomorrow's sunlight.
Lately, he often missed his stronger brother.
So, like the cedar man who offered fear new charms,
He whirls in the wind like bunch grass.

OWL SEEN IN REARVIEW MIRROR

It was a miracle he glimpsed owl swaying
Sideways through his eye. He watched it roll
Back into the hills, move on like glacial water;
Swing across the sky like a pendulum.
And does it follow stars through wheat fields
Because hunger is calling, or moon is so luminous?
Is sky then shaping this dreaming creature?
As is, it seems content to shift his roots,
Mirror his flight to snow. And how it pulls
Him into and out the car's back window
By the power of its agile, silent poetry.
Is he mouse paralyzed by its too perfect silence?
No artist, woman, nor dream, ever showed him this.
So he goes further, lets it drive him home,
Leave his soul soaring for the light of yellow moon.

THE DICE THROWER

Raven steals your name for an autumn joke—
Buries it under the thickest hemlock
Known to chipmunks. Too bad you were awake
For the event. He accuses you of asking
All the wrong questions over and over again.
You revolt to prove his medicine wheel's cracked.

He says your face is unmasked and madness
Has found a home. All animal, he calls you,
Claims you had a choice and forgot it.
Pain runs for the river, the river runs for wind.
He chuckles in the chattering darkness—
Turns you around until your shadow is the earth's.

TO LOVE

She and I alone step down the shore.
I hold her close because she loves the sea.
We watch boats cross the jetty's corridor.

The dark storm strikes our bodies with its lore
As the power of the wind we hear and feel.
She and I alone step down the shore.

The clouds that spark return the blue to force;
The rain drowns out the breakers' ebbing reefs.
We watch boats cross the jetty's corridor.

Kelp and cod are rooted to the shoal;
The terns dip green, turn shadow and are free.
She and I alone step down the shore.

This forest dream is a shield now transformed
The salt, the wind, the sun compose our dreams.
We watch boats cross the jetty's corridor.

When amber waves carve clam shells to the core,
We hear sandpiper from his cove of peace.
She and I alone step down the shore.
We watch boats cross the jetty's corridor.

HIS TEACHER

The comedian of bones is a bear of troubles,
Knocking the window to pieces, clawing out the room,

Entering my sleep as the uninvited guest, coy
As the woman who calls, asking how's my love life.

I groan, swear a little, drop the phone, turn left,
Then right, then over. So not to appear lost,

Baiting the wrong mouse, he taps the bedpost with his
Fanged necklace, goading me into facing the dancers,

Pain's tribe, wreathed in nettles, kelp, fish,
Bored with his reluctance to admit I've new fears,

I try to shame him with my death bundle; my only
Rattle. Then ask if I can return to the dream.

With eyes closed to regain exposed scars, I offer
Them to Cedar Bear, the one who fakes each promise,

Who crosses my name off his totem of white fog.

THE LEGEND OF OLD MAN

(for my grandfather, Francis Patsey)

Slipping into the Elwah river in winter offers fear.
This dawn, Old Man tells Raven to teach his child;
In the fern sun, he tells the boy of his father,
On a ship far beyond the village, beyond the cedars.
Alone, he sees his boy chasing the gulls,
Waiting for nothing but the morning star.

The silent grandfather forgot the morning star;
Caught by the river's pull, he sings for the child's fear;
Like sweet medicine, their fears meet the gulls.
He never speaks to the child
Now that each spring may split him like cedars;
The boy need never know the sea has lost his father.

Instead, he'll let him grow slowly to know his father,
When, one day, he'll stop beneath the morning star,
The night Raven will bury his cry in the cedars.
Then he'll say there's only love to handle fear,
The way this sunlight dances round the child,
The way his father named the storms with gulls.

Now Old Man lights his pipe; the flame burns gulls,
Yet, as if in dream, he sinks the ship; the father
Flies above the village to answer the child,
Erase the nightmare of a father stoned by morning star.
Cedar man lets fire burn down this fear,
The child running moons, the nightmare killing cedars.

Blue jay laughs at Old Man and child speaking to cedars;
Says, "The last man to fly died, a puzzle to gulls."
The child picks blackcaps to offer his fear.

Near the shore, he asks the sea to name his father.
Old Man is gone; the child waits for morning star.
As Trickster bears the tribe, the river bears the child.

"The mystery of your father is here my child—
When you leave our circle, these Klallam cedars,
Your father's journeys will meet your morning star."
The child smiles, and points, "Look, rainbow gulls!"
Old Man swats a fly, the child is his father.
They watch a raven drift home; its caw a dying fear.

A star washes down the mountain like a white fear.
Grandfather rises, throwing his story back to the cedars;
His grandson turns to the sea, calling the gulls.

II.

DIGGING OUT THE ROOTS

Worn flesh at last is history and treasure
Unto itself; its scars it still can keep,
Received from love, from memory's false measure,
From pain, from the long dream drawn back in sleep.

—Louise Bogan

DIGGING OUT THE ROOTS

Thirteen pieces of silver means bad luck,
If I think bad luck rolls thirteen ways,
And if I see the gambler, and not the forest.

Today I follow my spirit into the ruins
Of my Klallam ancestors, N'huia-wulsh,
Their white fir village, count the rainy seasons
Since grandfather fell in the brush like first cedar,
Where his flesh and bones settled in the dark
Regions of fern and snail. I return
To carve red moon out of my native sky.

Old Man canoeing on the Hoko river
Can mean much to a traveler who knows trouble
Is free and floating. Years and flights ago
This gentle grandfather, furious,
Struck me with a willow for defying him,
For fishing for rockfish that sang to agony
As I slapped their heads against the rocks.
The welts that appeared that blood-bright day
Are the songs embedded on my back and arms.

As a fern-shy boy in the Navy, I chained
Most of the voices of fear to coyote.
And as a minor drunk on legends from the sea,
I killed in delirium the Brig Warden
Who called me an idiot and a wetback.
But the ants of deliverance marched back into my blood
As those days shook me into manhood.

Home again, I meet a rare woman and we marry.
I watch her dry her thighs, by the yellow tub.
Her smile lights the walls with her dance,
The play of the kiss to dawn, and sleep.

We shared the labyrinths of two autumns,
Then, the scents of Seattle were alive,
Pine, rose, and maple, the sea a magic drummer,
Before the rain washed our dream out the window,
Leaving us two unknown statues.
The birth of a son our best poem.

Tossing the past back into the wine river,
I hid when the bottle crashed
Through the mirror and broke against my skull,
Before a new woman opened my eyes and I sighed,
When she whispered not to move,
So her hands could dance right down my back.

We painted our apartment light as the sun
Giving itself to a tahoma meadow;
Lived for its lake and swallows. I would
Carry her from the living room to our green bed,
Gently hold her warm breasts and body to my chest.

Neither she nor I remembered when or how the storm
Drove us far into the laughing mirror.
Having learned to love with irony,
We are careful and soft with the lights off.
Hearing music chip life off the moon,
No one can tell us our flesh will not wrinkle
Like paper, our bones not crack
With the logs in the winter fire.

We hunted for a ring, from city to train,
Window to valley, mountain to stream,
Then the clouds passed, leaving the wind and us
On a hill in waves of Scotch broom.

Not quite ready to carry the silence wheel,
Another failure flamed down her cheeks
To find its home in my heart,
The day our shadows attacked us like flies,
Chasing us down the subway to the street.

On each night Trickster mocked my totems,
I pushed my fist into nightmare's eye,
The window clown who mimed each wound again.
But panic let me alone when she handed
The cottage key to the ghosts of my wife and son.
Memory burns away the confusion of naming.

Walking under the sun of budding flowers,
There seem to be fewer errors to trust,
Humility to tear, songs to puzzle cedar hawk's descent;
And by summer's end, perhaps ocher wind
Will keep these feathers for an open field.

THE WAY

Myth lillies. A smog-edge sky blurs my eye
Like a cataract. The pond is abstract, a green
Ripple that flows through the frog. I discover
Wind has no direction, no word on summer.
I won't laugh at frog, if it won't laugh at me;
I've come to purge the fly-swarmed loneliness.
At thirty-three, it's neither self-indulgence
Nor a loser's plea to wear a freedom mask.
I'm maskless as the birch and half as white,
And glacier sun leaves me naked to the bone:
For cedar child lies grounded, opaque, invisible
As the traveler. So I wonder if I was
This boy who swam in Hoko river light to help
Moon find her feathers in the snowy pools.

READING THE MIRRORS OF
THE NAMELESS

Yes, father, you did hand me the charm,
Owl's rattle that will flicker you beyond
My footprints like Old Dreamer. And I announced
To sorrow, your totem's a Trickster joke—
An odious laugh that scatters your ashes,
Throws your cowardice to the Elder winds.
Listen, weasel without face, I'd drive you back
Each year to the day of your birth, with an arrow
Eagle sharpened on the dawn. For tonight, in my
Thirty-fifth year, my soul returned from roaming
The ruins, trying to find the cave where you hide.
Now it thanks my mother's aunt for giving me her
Father's name, that breaks you, the nameless mirror,
Turns your homeless lies as white as memory.

IN NEW YORK CITY

I'm here to speak to my father rapidly burying
The blood shields in the Hudson river mud;
The humorless fake runs in circles from
Mother's ancestors. And certainly the scars
I wear were earned, so I can ignore forever
The drunk's voice, my father's curse at his rejected
Name. And lately I've been a man of some fortune;
The women of the last few years have sung many
Secret poems to me, left my body warm wounds.
Friends have been family, shamans, elders,
Sons and daughters, totem carriers. So maybe
I'll try Salmon Berry Woman's feather charm,
Gift from a recent dream. "Your father," she said,
"Leave him in owl's cave, without light, shadow."

SONG TO FIRST WOMAN

I take the wrong road for the feel of its turning,
And the blind rooster perched on my shoulder
Croaks with joy. It's eagle's feather in the sand
To find I've nearly ended this search for my father's grave.
I need no more purge his indifference
Than a wolf needs the company of the dead. During
My body's best years I felt grief sapped my strength
Because of my mother's many-bladed bitchiness
When I was a child, a young man. Now the truth
Seems it was the terrible absence of my father,
And what's necessary is to act the man he wasn't,
See the only failure of dream and fantasy. From
This mound, to lie naked under snow, wait for First
Woman to offer me her eyes, the way to feed white
Buzzard the few remaining grains of my youth.

CARRIER OF THE WHEEL INTO WINTER

She runs down between the folds of herself,
After bringing him to her childhood's white beach.
Exhausted, she stops to hail the blue heron
Staring at the centerless pool
That ripples from its feet.
To leave the silence with the cold,
He kicks a pine cone clean of snow;
Circles the lake for its shield.
Thin wind voices rise sharply from the water;
Repeat the only sounds worth naming.

To meet her willingly at this edge,
He bends with the cattails to hear her song's refrain,
Again, offers the woman she wants to drown
Another way to bury scars.

To help her believe there is something left,
He vows to remember every night
He slept in the fields of her eyes.
Thus he reaches to catch her hand,
Show her returning spirit his other open hand.
For him, she carries winter's wheel before the dark.

FOOL'S CRANE SPINS THE WATER WHEEL FOR YOU

(for Martha, on her birthday)

You are cedar woman who shakes the stars both
Day and night. You clap and dance for memory
When sorrow runs naked down your nerves.
You reach the edge where day begins to drift,
Then pour rainbow colors through your fingers.
Later, you close your eyes as you pass the beggars
Who call you, those men who want to bury
Their failures into your breasts like teeth.

Look up, look up, I am the village jester
Come to lead you from their bitter beaks—
Hand you a torch of night flaming pitch
To blind those enemies of pity and love.
O hear my rattle, watch this medicine trade
Dawn, the path back to your name's beginning.

POEMS FOR THE WOMAN WHO FLED

"It's not your spirit I find incompatible,
But the day-to-day ups and downs."

1.

I open the window to see rain's several faces—
Tap a final message of farewell to you,
Do my sun dance through your eyes on the river.
In your honor and my faith, cynic sat across
From me, exchanged the masks, the lies, the bodies,
Love's cruelties, then shrugged, and said, that's
Politics, but wouldn't we do it, do it all again!
I'm not foolish, but a fool, and wolf's my father.
Tonight, you wouldn't believe the moon's descent
Down Mount Takoma. The crimson clouds play rainbow,
Look so close, I can almost understand their
Reasons for vanishing in the ocean. O Natalie,
When you left me the memory of your green eyes,
A white wind from Alaska blurred this empty house.

2.

I hear your final letter close the gate
On me, when I run for your voice, the lake's
Green loon. And who watches you hurl my rage
Into this mirror like a miniature Stonehenge?
If it's my totem, I ask for a sounder drumming
Back to orange moon's field. The crowd
That forces me back to the street never says
Why you aren't here, why you never heard
Before cedar man's lament. And the wounds collect
The ways to exit through the door, the lock,
The key, but the terrors are terrible detractors,

And leave the fingers hanging in the glove with no pain.
So tomorrow I bury the blue jay who wears
Your name like a necklace of moonlight.

   3.
You whisper threats that I'm not dreaming, speak
In tongues as pointed as mosquito's. Nightmare's fire,
You say, and to prove it, beat my face with nettle wings.
Your jests are those of fog's drifting warriors,
And when you offer me the sight of your blind god,
Too easily change my shadow to fit the joke.
I plead this is no way to treat an insomniac,
And recoil into a cedared knot, frozen in its eye.
Hopelessly, I argue for the right to fail alone,
But you claim I'm here for your amusement, not mine.
With one wing around the woman who fled, the other,
Me, you say you're tried of begging for my life;
Deny you packed her clothes, shoved her out the door,
Laugh when I admit she's still dying in my heart.

III.

A CYCLE FOR THE WOMAN IN THE FIELD

He who loses his dreaming is lost.

—Australian Aborigine

SECRET MEETING

I make my zigzag way through the night
With the blackest stars
The street-lights cannot hide,
Think of you by the lake,
The night Center Moon wind
Called us to the shore to mute our memories
With the duck's wild courting.
Woman, I have not yet returned to my shadow,
Sleeping under the moontree like a child.

HER SONG IS THE GIFT

Snow plays down the weekend of the city,
Silencing the chatter of people,
Cars, sudden winds, as if opening
The window to your absence. When I am morning's
Naked clown, your sweet body
Will catch me asleep, when
The geese cry, Spring! Spring!

LAST NIGHT I GLIMPSED THE MOON, LISTENING TO HER STONES

I fly out the window to sit on the wire,
Add a new voice to the telephone,
Drink rain, search for the woman
Who runs naked through my field, fall
Through nights down the winter we gave away.
If you ask why I left,
My house will find a home in your memory.

GOODBYE

Don't ask me what is found in history.
I have been a stranger on these streets
For seven bottles now. The police
Whistle has the ward on missing persons.
This morning, not even the homeless
Dog I barked to answered back.
Never again will the East stone my solitude.

HAS THE STORM PASSED?

I step like a child past the avenue crowd,
Later, am an old man who trades
Jokes with the park blue jays.
Sitting on the bench, the rain
Washes me into the eye of Spring.
A moment ago, a gypsy moon exploded
The peacock's call. Sometimes
A dream woman sleeps with you,
Brushes her hands across the fern's green fire.

CELEBRATING THE CENTER MOON

The stars, a willow riverbank—
Nearby, a crow watches for yellow grains to bloom.
For the next three nights,
I will teach my scars to drink like clowns,
In the maple darkness, where heron,
Gliding over the marsh,
Vanishes at the edge of the watery plains.

MUSIC

I listen to her heart retreat.
Hyacinths are riding on the windmill of the moon.
I am a stone bedding down in the stream;
She bathes in the unmarked waters of my solitude.
Will she hear my song chanting in the dawn?

THANKING SOME ELDER POETS

When feelings of self-pity
Crawl down my back like a rose-spider,
I remember your parodies of the sentimentalist,
Feel ashamed. And only when I live
The failure, am I once more
A man of seed.

RUNNER FOR THE CLOUDS AND RAIN

I am the fox roaming for your changes.
I am the salmon dreaming in the waters of the sun.
I am the mushroom celebrating rains.
I am the bear dancing for the gentle woman.
I am the guardian of the infant child.
I am the carrier of the Elders' song.
I run for the dead and the rainbow!

TO AWAKE

My heart is an elk grazing in the meadow
She called our healing ground.
I am so entangled in her sweet grass,
That if she opened her eyes while asleep,
She would see me lying joyfully
In the sunlight of her young ferns.

THE WHEEL OF RETURN

I dig up and quickly bury every old mistake,
To stay alive behind my snowy shield.
A fugitive from suicide,
I hunt for legends from the sky,
Whirling in its hands,
The lost doubts of the epileptic.
I am determined to reach
The labyrinth of the open window,
Where you blossom like an orange chrysanthemum.
Everything rests in the field of your echo.

CLOSING CIRCLES

Not wanting to be an enemy of Baltimore,
I invite it to take a walk,
Work things out, trade poems, puns, failures.
Hailing the gate-keeper to strangers,
I make a hermit of memory, and she
Drinks from my cup, eases our resignation.

I stop at the vanishing point of the rainbow.
Suddenly it is the morning of eclipse,
And you gaze into the green tapestry
Of the white firs, where I stand alone in your eye,
A hummingbird who dances for your hand.

IV.
DANCING EAGLE TO SLEEP

The road beside the school goes either way.
The last bell rings. You run again,
The only man going your direction.

—Richard Hugo

DANCING EAGLE TO SLEEP

Your past and mine. Two countries lying
On a bed of rose and stone.

As children we shimmered through adolescence
Doing the electric teddybear rag,
Turned tiger's growl at the first circus
Into textbook pages that left the teacher
In the boredom room. Then we piped
A caravan of songs to her from the streets,
Animals and all.

Yellow, blue, and green clowns leap for joy
Through three summer hoops.
Can any laughing spirit be more game?
We spin around the next corner on a memory top.

Are these the strings needed to bind the scars?
Then will cricket rave about blue jay?
Outside, a violence as opaque as a watch
Ties us to its face. The city
Forgets to dream, exiles its clowns,
Buries its women under the white tomb
That reflects neither the sinking
Nor the cries of the desperate chorus.

Shaking off the rubble, we hope
To find the poem again while asleep.

By traveling with an ear to the wind,
A hand in the dirt, we smell the roses tossing
Golden in the field. It strengthens

Us like a cup of wine, slows the disintegration
Down so we hear the last chord
From the gypsy's blue guitar.

We make a soft bed of the orange descent,
Catch the few remaining beats
That put eagle to sleep, open us to what
The window has imagined.

WINTER MOON

Breathing in air crisp as spun frost,
Wind has possession of our nerves,
Our hands that are the running
Ground for snowflakes. Retreating deeper
Into the evening sunset, we step
Through a rose's tumbling past,
Still as vermillion as our unmarked meadow.
Now we are guests of white crow, oak;
Chickadee, picking berries glazed with ice,
Unaware of two thorned beggars sliding by.

TO A YOUNG WOMAN FROM PASCO

With patience I learn to hear the river flow
Inward, follow your soul vanishing in the rapids,
Hear your secret echo through the canyon;
Your body pulls me to your side like the moon.

I'm pleasantly passive as you drive; listen to your
Past adventures, the names of surrounding hills,
The declaration we can only be friends,
But that you'll lie with me once, after you set
The spring twilight sparrow in my hands.
Now climbing with ease, your fingers lightly dance

Over blossom and stem, opening your body to its fire.
When you point to the moss and fern meadow ahead,
I run to meet your spirit lying in the grass,
Find your name beneath the fragrance of your skin.

THE HERMIT

(after Kosinski's novel, The Painted Bird)

Without family, he appeared one morning in the village,
Hunched over his past like an abandoned crane.
He was through with wandering from nest to tree,
Forest to village. His name was Lekh, keeper of birds.
When he reached the alders, the Middle Ages,
To hunt for Ludmila's lair, the sensualist,
Each step drove desire a little deeper into his heart,
Brought him closer to the mirage,
The clearing where the scars bloomed marigold.

The villagers called him half bird, half tree, soulless,
And placed bets on whether the devil sent him
To mock their already haunted lives.
Safely hidden behind moss and fern, the children
Would stare at the man of knotted pine and claw,
Hum his songs offering snow fools the dream.

Rumor spread slowly about Lekh's retreat.
Suddenly, as if enraged by silence,
Ludmila's indifference, he began to paint his birds
Multi-colors, rainbow hues, set them free to die.

After tossing the last memory into the blood-hot sky,
He was last seen running from his hut
For the river, to rip the clothes from his body
That named him Lekh, spit one last time
At the ghosts who had devoured his mind like ants.

ODE TO TOUCHING

Outside, another wind sands the chestnut mirror
To brown dust, throwing leaf puzzles
Down night's window fall:
The winter clown that peels off our masks.
Although we have given ourselves to the sun,
Tonight we plant seeds on the moon,
Flat as a silver dollar.

The candle burns through the table,
Chair, books, and us,
Leaves our whispers alone
To make their way out the door,
Carried on our rippling explosions
To become two small stones in the grass.
As usual, asking no one's forgiveness,

Silence splinters last year's song,
Crystallizes the few remaining forms
Like seven-year-old paint,
Easily unnerving us when the speakers
Disintegrate our age. Now separated
From your touch by this ghost,
I threaten to tie a pun around its neck

Until it hollers I'm your last hallucination.
After roaming my hands over your sweet breasts,
My lips over your ears, I catch faintly
Your even breath, feel dawn warm your nakedness,
As we slip off into sleep's terrible rainbow.

THE RUINS

A languid sun penetrates the smog;
January hums an old tune, and we follow.
Having pulled ourselves from the last wreck
On the road, we call the sparrow that calls tomorrow.
The wars outside pick the day's puzzles,
Stack plastic and glass accusers at the door,
Headline mimics of our crashing steel apocalypse.

Seattle's eroding gray edge eats away
The cottage day and night. The children along
The sidewalks do not wave or speak any more;
Instead they hurl stones at their shadows.
Even the elders turn their backs as we
Walk an earth they abandon with the raven.

Ending an august evening in an alley of roses,
Our bodies search for the rhythms to these ruins;
The old selves make their feeble claims.
It's the shoes that wear us out.
We run for the garden shared with the blind.

North wind returns with rain beating the rains;
Collects its little amusements from the inlet Sound.
Imitating the spirits hiding under leaves,
We hold ourselves deep inside our hands.

ISLAND IN THE HEART OF CROW

Wind and cliff offer us crows flying into dunes.
On this coastal crescent, our fumbling love
Burrows with the fleas into August sand.
You arrive to strengthen shield, dance, the stones;
Teach my nerves how to carry your parents' scorn,
The island creatures covering every footprint.
You promise confusion an easy descent into echoes.
When running my hands through your tossing hair,
Your body burns the sunlight down my spine,
Pulling my blood skyward to bloom with the poor.
When your eyes rest in mine, give back my life,
We will survive the avalanche of mistakes
Like these waves leaving us the island's heart
Whirling our hands steadily toward earth.

TESS ONE WINTER IN THE FIELDS

She watches a snowflake melt against her palm,
Feels the snow settle on the ground, coarsen her mood.
Some townsmen shudder at this ghostly blizzard,
Its drifts deepening the death of their closing year.
Ice tufts cup the hedgerow's thorns;
Make them look four times their actual size.
This white terrain flows crystal in their blood.
She hears the men brooding: something must be wrong.

Cobwebs hanging for life along stone walls reveal
Fine lines where they are usually concealed.
A haze leaves the fields birch white, then falls
Like loops of silk around the barn and plough.
Because the snow now curdles into slush,
Scarecrow tips his hat to wind and cow.
Suddenly, birds circle from the frozen North.
Huge shabby birds with eyes both black and bright.

She wonders, will these creatures carry some nightmare
Her town of Flintcomb Ash will soon imagine?
When the sky's struck by these brazen birds,
She and another maid under their beating wings
Dismiss their feathered strangeness with a shrug,
For they aretired of digging in this soil,
Where wind changes only the cow's bell in the field.

POEM TO A GYPSY WOMAN

I pass the nights reading the ways we opened—
Reach the alcove where you tossed magnolia blossoms
To fox running from shadow to shadow in your name.

Since you left to kiss the youths you'll never find,
I throw an empty bottle through the cottage window.
Recovering slowly, I shake off the glass,
Give the heart another breath, move on.

Snow bites into the lake, cattails, chickadees, and me.
Yet, it is this walk that helps regain my silence,
Glimpse the end of the icy road,
Repeat the failure without you.
Here snowman is companion to your dance;
Your hair curled in his hands that can't let go.

I imagine the geese as scattering white blossoms,
To settle in the afternoon
You were a dazzling flame in my arms,
Then watch this creature darken each flake,
Drown memory's fickle message.

Do you remember when the brute pounded man-child
To the ground, who also dreamed of his first mistake?
That this stranger added his nightmare to the wall?
May we still hide out, make love, regain the other world?

In my retreat, the crows call out your name:
A water mandala, a loss, giving me this labyrinth;
A kite I sail into willow hills, yellow lupine.

I am night's Trickster saying if you want the blood,
The pulse, the body, play the wheel of lust again,
Return and find me writing elegies in the sand.

Reaching my cottage, the end of a bitter week,
Dawn wonders about you no more than I.
And though I am only one more stumbling fool,
You still raise my cedar soul.

So, if we meet tomorrow, next year, or never—
Know I hope to swim beside your body;
Touch your red rainbow hair;
The moon lighting my steps
Without stars, past the ducks drifting to sleep,
Past the fox burying my desire in the snow.

About the author

Duane Niatum was born in 1938, in Seattle, Washington. He is an American Indian, a member of the Klallam tribe whose ancestral lands border the Washington Coast along the Strait of Juan de Fuca. His early life was spent in Washington, Oregon, California, and Alaska. He joined the Navy at seventeen, spending two years of his enlistment in Japan. On his return, he later graduated from the University of Washington with a B.A. in English, and afterward received his M.A. from The Johns Hopkins University.

His poetry has been nourished by his increasing interest in painting, sculpture and music as well as by his exposure to Oriental cultures. "There are parallels between American Indian and Oriental philosophies and arts which gave me an interesting hybrid way of looking at things. I learned restraint, how to hold back, to understate both the object and the feeling for the object. This is one of the best influences I could have had. I am grateful."

The other major influence reflected in his poems in his Indian ancestry. "My roots are in the earth and sky philosophies and arts of my ancestors. As a child, my grandfather and great-uncle taught me always to humble my soul before the spiritual reality of things as well as man."

Duane Niatum's poetry has previously been published in *The Nation*, *Prairie Schooner*, *Northwest Review*, and many other literary journals and anthologies.

This is his third collection of poems, the most recent being *Ascending Red Cedar Moon*.